world tour
India

RESHMA SAPRE

www.raintreepublishers.co.uk
Visit our website to find out more information about Raintree books.

To order:
☎ Phone 44 (0) 1865 888112
▤ Send a fax to 44 (0) 1865 314091
▢ Visit the Raintree Bookshop at **www.raintreepublishers.co.uk** to browse our catalogue and order online.

First published in Great Britain by Raintree Publishers, Halley Court, Jordan Hill, Oxford, OX2 8EJ, part of Harcourt Education.
Raintree is a registered trademark of Harcourt Education Ltd.

Editorial: Sally Knowles
Cover Design: Peter Bailey and Michelle Lisseter
Production: Jonathan Smith

Printed and bound in China and Hong Kong by South China Printing Company

ISBN 1 844 21306 4
07 06 05 04 03
10 9 8 7 6 5 4 3 2 1

British Library Cataloguing in Publication Data
Sapre, Reshma
India (World Tour)
954
A full catalogue for this book is available from the British Library.

Acknowledgements
The publishers would like to thank the following for permission to reproduce photographs:
p. **1a** ©Dennis Cox/D.E. Cox Photo Library; p. **1c** ©Bob Krist/eStock; p. **3a** ©Bob Krist/eStock; p. **5** ©Dave Bartuff/CORBIS; p. **7** ©Arthur ThEvenart/CORBIS; p. **8** ©Bettmann/CORBIS; p. **13a** ©Tiziana and Gianni Baldizzone/CORBIS; p. **13b** ©Jeremy Horner/CORBIS; p. **14** ©Andrea Pistolesi/Getty Images; p. **15** ©AFP/CORBIS; p. **16** ©Paul Harris/Getty Images; p. **19** ©Dinodia Pitcure Agency; p. **21a** ©Joel Simon/Getty Images; p. **23a** ©Kamal Kishore/Reuters/TimePix; p. **23b** ©World Pictures/eStock; p. **25** ©Frans Lemmens/Getty Images; p. **27a** ©Vishnu Panjabi/SuperStock; p. **28** ©Baldev Kapoor/SuperStock; p. **29** ©Reuters NewMedia Inc/CORBIS; p. **31a** ©Cary Wolinski/ Aurora; p. **31b** ©Earl and Nazima Kowall/CORBIS; p. **33** ©Dennis Cox/D.E. Cox Photo Library; pp. **34,35** ©StockFood; p. **37** ©Catherine Karnow/CORBIS; p. **38a** ©Dinodia Picture Agency; p. **38b** ©Jeff Rotman; p. **40** ©AFP/CORBIS; p. **41** ©Roman Soumar/CORBIS; p. **42** ©Paul Harris/Getty Images; p. **43b** ©Tiziana and Gianni Baldizzone/CORBIS; p. **44a** ©Wallace Kirkland/TimePix; p. **44b** ©eStock Photo; p. **44c** ©Ted Streshinsky/CORBIS.

Additional Photography by Comstock Royalty Free, Corbis Royalty Free, Getty Images Royalty Free, and the Steck-Vaughn Collection.

Cover photography: Background: Getty Images/Taxi/Peter Adams. Foreground: Getty Images/Stone/Nicholas De Vore

Contents

Welcome to India

If you want to travel to an exciting country and meet new and different people, visiting India will open your eyes to an exciting **culture** and its customs. In this book you will learn about battling gods, ancient temples and flourishing **empires**. You will be introduced to a country with a fabulous landscape. India has high mountains, vast deserts filled with unusual animals and bustling cities with plenty to see and do.

Tips to get you started

• Look at the pictures

This book has lots of great photos. Flip through and look at the pictures you like best. This is a good way to get an idea of what this book is all about. Read the captions to learn more about the photos.

• Use the glossary

As you read this book, you may notice that some words appear in **bold** print. Look up bold words in the glossary on page 46. The glossary will help you learn what the words mean.

• Use the index

If you are looking for information on a specific topic, then you might want to go to the index on page 48. The index has a list of all the subjects that are covered in the book.

▲ SHIPS OF THE DESERT
People who need to get around the desert in India often ride on camels. Camels are sometimes known as the 'ships of the desert'.

India's past

If you want to get to know India well, take some time to learn about India's history. Many different cultures have played a role in developing Indian society. India started with only one culture, but has become a country with various religions, languages and ways of life.

Ancient history

The first Indian **civilization** lived along the Indus Valley for more than a thousand years, from around 3500 BC. The rulers were priests who practised an early form of Hinduism. They are known as the Early Dravidians.

In about 1500 BC, invaders called the Aryans pushed the Dravidians south. The Aryans brought their own forms of religion and politics to India. To this day, Indians can be classified by their ancient **heritage** as Dravidian Indian or Aryan Indian. The way of life in modern India is a combination of these two civilizations.

The Aryans introduced the **Vedic tradition** and the ancient language called **Sanskrit**. They also introduced the **caste system**. A caste is the social

◄ GREAT GANESHA
This is a statue of the Hindu god known as Lord Ganesha. He has the head of an elephant. Ganesha is said to guide souls in the right direction.

▲ **THE RED FORT**
The British army once occupied this historic building. The Red Fort now stands for India's independence. Every year on India's Independence Day the prime minister gives a speech there.

group into which a person was born and it cannot change. Castes go from very high to very low. The poorer people of India are usually in the lower castes. Buddhism, another religion, started in India in about 500 BC.

Several Indian emperors fought wars to control parts of the country. There are many different **ethnic groups** in India because of all these wars. In 1192, many people in the north became Muslim.

European traders came to India in search of rare spices. They used the famous spice trade route, a path used by European traders to travel to India and China to buy spices, which they took back to Europe to sell. By the 1500s the Portuguese, Dutch, Danish and French all had **trading posts** set up in different parts of India.

▲ PROTEST FOR PEACE
Mohandas Gandhi (on the right) was called The Mahatma, meaning 'Great Soul', because of his peaceful leadership. Above, he meets supporters during his hunger strike.

The beginning of modern times

India was ruled by the Mughal empire during the 16th and 17th centuries. In 1610, the British East India company established a trading outpost, and by 1769 had gained control of all European trade in India. In 1858, the British government took control of all British

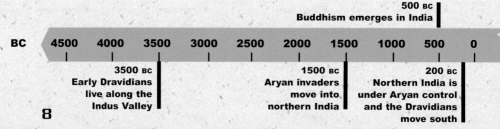

500 BC
Buddhism emerges in India

| BC | 4500 | 4000 | 3500 | 3000 | 2500 | 2000 | 1500 | 1000 | 500 | 0 |

3500 BC
Early Dravidians
live along the
Indus Valley

1500 BC
Aryan invaders
move into
northern India

200 BC
Northern India is
under Aryan control
and the Dravidians
move south

8

interests in India. India lived under British rule for a long time. The country changed because of the British **influence**.

After World War I, many Indians wanted to fight for freedom. But under the guidance of a man called Mohandas Gandhi, they decided not to fight. Gandhi became the leader of the Indian National Congress Party. He led a non-violent **revolt** against the British.

At this time, there were two main religious groups in India – the Hindus and the Muslims. The Muslims did not want to give up power to the Hindus, but there were more Hindus than Muslims in India by then.

In 1947, India became an independent **republic**. Part of the country split away to form a new country called Pakistan. Most Indian Muslims went to live there.

India today

Muslims and Hindus still fight each other in some disputed areas. There are some places in India that are not safe for travellers because of fighting.

India has different states with different languages. There are eighteen languages. Hindi and English are the main languages and most business is done in English.

1500
European trading posts start to develop

1610s
The British establish trading posts

1858
India comes under British rule

0   500   1000   1500   1600   1700   1800   1900   2000   AD

1192
Muslims arrive from the Middle East

1947
India gains independence

A look at India's geography

Since ancient times, India has been known as a land of changes. Tourists travelling through India can visit empty desert or lush jungle. There are many different types of wildlife to look out for. India has king cobras, tigers, elephants, monitor lizards and, of course, peacocks – the national bird.

Land

The Republic of India, or Bharat (the national name), is the seventh-largest country in the world. The whole country is about thirteen times larger than the United Kingdom, but with more than 1000 million people living there, people live a lot closer together.

The high peaks of the Himalaya Mountains mark the northern border of India. The Himalayas attract trekkers and skiers. The Indian Ocean lines India's southern coasts. If you enjoy relaxing on the beach, you will find resorts on both the Arabian Sea and the Bay of Bengal. Snorkelling, scuba diving and swimming can be lots of fun in the Bay of Bengal, near the city of Goa or off the coast of one of the Andaman or Nicobar islands.

Camels are a popular form of transport in the Thar Desert. A camel ride can last for a few hours or a few days, but a guide is essential to avoid getting lost in the desert – it's 259,000 square kilometres (100,000 square miles) of emptiness.

Reader's tip: Use the map to locate all the countries that border India.

INDIA'S SIZE ▶

India spans an area of 3,287,590 sq km (1,269,338 sq miles). It also includes more than 300 islands in the Arabian Sea, the Bay of Bengal and the Indian Ocean. India borders the countries of Pakistan, China, Nepal, Bhutan, Bangladesh, Myanmar and Sri Lanka.

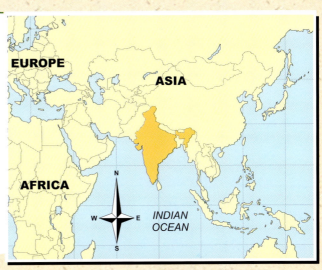

Water

The Indian Ocean, the Bay of Bengal and the Arabian Sea surround much of India. The Indian Ocean is the third-largest ocean in the world. The Bay of Bengal is a good place for fishing or trade. To the west is the Arabian Sea.

India has three main rivers – the Indus, the Ganga, or Ganges, and the Brahmaputra. They all flow from the Himalayas. The Ganga is the longest river in India. It flows for 2510 kilometres (1560 miles). The Hindus believe that the Ganga is a **sacred** river, so there are often very long queues to get to its shore. This river is believed to be the goddess Ganga as she appears on the Earth. Hindus believe that bathing in the Ganga can wash away all their sins.

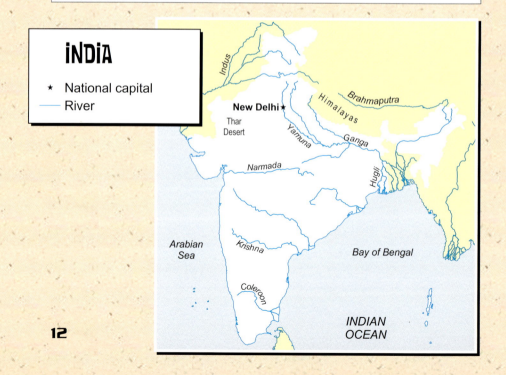

INDIA

★ National capital
— River

Indus

New Delhi ★

Thar Desert

Himalayas

Brahmaputra

Yamuna

Ganga

Narmada

Hugli

Arabian Sea

Krishna

Bay of Bengal

Coleroon

INDIAN OCEAN

▲ LIFE ALONG THE BRAHMAPUTRA
Fishermen may have problems during the monsoon season. Heavy rains make the river overflow and cause flooding.

THE GANGA – A DYING RIVER? ▶
Scientists fear that the sacred river Ganga is slowly dying. Its natural environment is being destroyed by pollution.

◀ **NORTHERN PEAKS**
**By early December,
northern cities start
to get colder.**

Climate

There are three seasons in India – the hot, the wet and
the cool. It is never very cold in India unless you are up
on a snowy mountain in the north. The coldest it
usually gets is about 16°C.

The warm air starts to flow into India in February. By
April, it can get so hot that it is very uncomfortable. The
temperatures are from 30 to 40°C. After May, you will
need to watch out for the thunderstorms and rain.
However, this rainy weather is nothing compared to the
famous Indian **monsoon** season. Monsoons are strong
winds that cause a change of season. In India, the
monsoons bring very heavy rains which can do a lot of
damage. Even with all this rain, the weather does not get
much cooler in the south.

▲ **THERE IS NO ESCAPING A MONSOON**
The monsoons begin in June and last until October. For four months, heavy rains and winds move from the south up the north-east coast of India.

kolkata: snapshot of a big city

▲ BUSY CITY
Central Kolkata is packed with shops and people.

Kolkata's old English name was Calcutta. Kolkata is the second-largest city in India after Mumbai (Bombay), with nearly 13 million people. It's a busy place, with trains, aeroplanes and buses going all over India. There is plenty to see in Kolkata, making it the perfect place to begin a journey through India. Kolkata is also famous for its festivals and celebrations.

City facts

An Englishman **founded** Kolkata in 1690. It was known as the second city of the British Empire. Where does the name Kolkata, or Calcutta, come from? No one is really sure, but some think the city was named after the Hindu goddess Kali. Others think the name came from 'kali kata', a reference to the local art of producing limestone from burnt snail shells.

East of the river Hugli

Kolkata lies on the easternmost coast of India, next to Bangladesh. It is the home of the Howrah Bridge. This bridge is used by everyday travellers and for moving trade goods across the river Hugli. The Howrah Bridge is the busiest bridge in the world. It was opened to traffic in 1943 and offers a superb view of Kolkata.

Once you cross the bridge, take time to enjoy the busy Howrah District. There you will find Howrah Railway Station, a distinctive red brick building with eight square towers. It serves as the heart of transport in and out of this region. It was built in 1906 and is an amazing piece of **architecture**.

West of the Hugli

While in Kolkata, you can visit the Botanical Gardens. These gardens are the largest and oldest in India. Founded in 1786, they host more than 30,000 varieties of plant and tree. One of the most famous trees in the Botanical Gardens is an ancient banyan tree that is 250 years old. This tree has a **canopy** 396 metres wide. If you want to see India's famous lotus flowers, you can see these lovely plants floating in the gardens' **lagoons**.

If you like history, then visit the Indian Museum, where ancient **artefacts** are on display. Next, investigate the famous Kali Temple. Kali is the most feared of the Hindu gods and goddesses because she is the goddess of destruction and rebirth.

HOWRAH STATION ▶
You can travel to almost anywhere in India from Howrah Station. Most Indians travel by train, so this is one of the world's busiest railway stations.

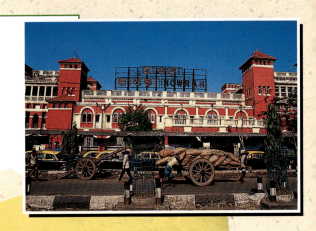

KOLKATA'S TOP-TEN CHECKLIST

If you are going to Kolkata, here is a list of ten things you have to do.

- ☐ Learn about ancient India at the Indian Museum.
- ☐ Cross the Howrah Bridge and take in the view.
- ☐ Look down at the skyline of Kolkata from the Vidyasagar Setu.
- ☐ Visit the Kali Temple to watch Hindu rituals.
- ☐ Take pictures of the flowers and trees in the Botanical Gardens.
- ☐ Stand in the shade of the enormous, 250-year-old banyan tree.
- ☐ Take a ferry across the river Hugli for a picnic.
- ☐ Take a train from Howrah Station.
- ☐ Try to learn some words in Bengali, the language of Kolkata.
- ☐ Go to the cinema and enjoy some spicy Indian food.

Four top sights

India has a lot to offer. It is useful to decide what you would like to see before you go. Here is a list to help you get started.

The Taj Mahal

When visiting India, every traveller should see the Taj Mahal. Located in the city of Agra, the Taj Mahal is one of the wonders of the world. The emperor Shah Jahan built it in memory of his wife. The construction of the building began in 1631 and didn't finish until 1653.

The emperor's wife, Mumtaz Mahal, died while giving birth. Legend says that the emperor was so heartbroken that his hair went grey overnight.

The Taj Mahal may be the most magnificent structure ever made in the name of love. The monument has a very high dome shape and is made entirely out of marble. It is covered with semi-precious stones that are actually set into the marble. The Taj Mahal is an amazing work of architecture and cannot be missed.

There are other wonderful dome monuments and **mausoleums** in Agra. These structures, as well as the Taj Mahal, display the best of Indian architecture.

▲ ROYAL TOUR
Indian women begin their tour of the Taj Mahal. There are several different buildings to explore, as well as beautiful gardens.

◀ THE TAJ MAHAL
The Taj Mahal appears to float in the mist at dawn. It is one of the world's great wonders.

The Eternal City

Varanasi, or the Eternal City, has been the religious centre of India for more than 2000 years. The Hindu religion is a very important part of Indian history. Many of India's monuments and sites are dedicated to the Hindu gods and goddesses.

Varanasi was once called Benares. It is one of the most sacred places in the world for Hindus who believe it is the city where the gods Shiva and Parvati stood when time first began. Varanasi is also mentioned in the Hindu **epic** tale, the Mahabharata. This adventure tells of dragons, monsters and powerful gods.

Varanasi was built on the banks of the sacred Ganga. It has many historic temples to visit. People of all races make **pilgrimages** to the Eternal City. It is an important place of learning for Indians.

On the banks of the Ganga, you can watch people take ritual baths in the river, or practise yoga on the shore. Yoga involves special breathing exercises and stretches. Many people find it very calming.

While in Varanasi, it is interesting to take a boat ride. There is a special trip down the river at dawn, a sacred time to Hindus.

Another good place to visit is the Sarnath. This is the Buddhist centre. Afterwards, be sure to go to the Golden Temple and, later, shop for fabric or a **sitar**.

◀ **BATHING IN THE GANGA**
People have come here for centuries. They purify their souls by bathing in the sacred Ganga.

▲ **GHATS**
Special stairways called ghats lead to the river.

Jaipur

Jaipur is called the Pink City. All of the old buildings and city walls in Jaipur have a natural pink tint. The warm colour makes Jaipur a welcoming place for any visitor. At night, the pink stone makes the city seem to glow.

An Indian astronomer designed the city with wide streets in a rectangular pattern. Jaipur is home to the famous Johari Bazaar. If you like fine jewellery, then Johari Bazaar is the place to shop. India is known for its unique jewellers and designs.

If you are looking for a good place to take some photos, make sure you go to the Hawa Mahal, or Palace of the Winds. The Hawa Mahal overlooks the entire city of Jaipur. It has a wonderful view because it was built in 1799 so the ladies of the royal household could look down across this lovely city.

▲ **PALACE OF THE WINDS**
The Hawa Mahal was dedicated to the Indian god Krishna. It has an open-air observatory from which people can look at the stars.

Darjeeling

Famous for its tea, the city of Darjeeling is also a good holiday spot with an incredible view of the Himalaya mountains. It has a large variety of exotic plants and a waterfall that is breathtaking. British troops based in India in the mid–1800s used to go to Darjeeling for rest and relaxation, to escape the heat of the lowlands.

Darjeeling sits along a high ridge in the Himalayas. It has a chairlift called the Passenger Ropeway. The Ropeway is like a ski lift which goes from Darjeeling to the shopping area along the river Little Ranjit.

The nearby Zoological Park is one of the best places to see some of India's wildlife. There are Siberian tigers, snow leopards and rare red pandas. Siberian tigers are **endangered**. A lot of the land that the tigers lived on has been taken for farming, and so the tigers have lost their habitat and and sources of food. As a result, the number of tigers has fallen, and some hungry tigers have attacked humans.

Darjeeling tea is drunk all over the world, and there are lots of tea plantations here. A plantation is like a large farm. If you have ever wondered how tea is made, visit the Happy Valley Tea Estate. Here you will be able to watch a lesson in tea production and then sample some of the tea that they grow there. 'Taking tea' is a national pastime in India. A national pastime is something many people in a certain place do to relax or have fun. There are lots of opportunities for visitors to try some of India's famous tea.

▲ **MOUNTAINS OF TEA**
Tea pickers climb high in the mountains of Darjeeling
to pick its world-famous tea.

RED PANDAS ▶
Red pandas are rare.
Adult red pandas grow
only slightly larger
than a domestic cat.

Going to school in India

Only half of the children in India go to school. Most boys and girls go to work in factories at an early age. Many poor families cannot send their children to school. Girls are less likely to go to school than boys are. India has one of the highest **illiteracy** rates in the world – many people cannot read or write. Some children can leave their factory jobs and start school between the ages of seven and fourteen. They may go to small schools where they sit on the floor.

Children of wealthier families attend school from an early age and often go on to university. Their schools are more modern, and Indian universities are among the best in the world.

▲ **AN INDIAN CLASSROOM**
Students gather for their daily lessons in a small school for boys and girls.

Indian sports

The most popular sport in India is cricket. It is played by people all over the country. There have been many famous international cricketers from India including Kapil Dev, who was named 'Indian cricketer of the 20th century', Sunil Gavaskar and Sachin Tendulkar.

Many Indians also play field hockey. Field hockey is India's national game. Modern field hockey was created in England and was introduced to India in the 19th century. India has won eight gold medals for hockey at the Olympic Games.

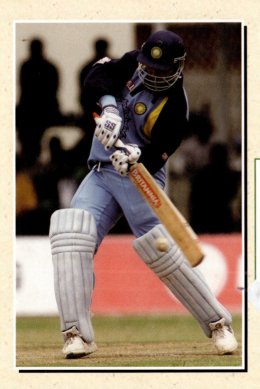

◀ **CRICKET**
Introduced by the British, cricket has become a national pastime in India. India won the cricket World Cup in 1993.

From farming to factories

Many Indians live off the land as farmers. India's vast area makes it easy to grow many different types of produce. Food is a big part of India's **economy**, and the country **imports** almost as much as it **exports**. India is very famous for its spices. It exports spices such as saffron and coriander all over the world.

India is also known for its large **textile** industry. Clothing and fabrics are big business in this nation. Indian factories also produce steel products for export. Many Indians work in jewel mines and exotic gemstones are used for making jewellery. Jewellery sales bring many rupees into Indian businesses. The rupee is the currency used in India.

As well as working in farms and factories, people in India do the same types of jobs that people do anywhere else in the world. There are lawyers, plumbers, journalists and so on. However, Indians are probably best known for their outstanding work in technology and healthcare. More and more Indians now work in the computer industry. There are also many Indian students training to become doctors.

FASCINATING FACT
Saffron, or kesar as it is called in India, is the most expensive spice in the world. It takes 165,000 flowers to produce just 1 kilogram (2.2 pounds) of the spice. Just imagine a field of that many flowers, for so little spice.

▲ INDIAN FACTORIES...
India is one of the world's biggest textile and clothing manufacturers.

... AND INDIAN FARMS ▶
These women are picking saffron.

The Indian government

The Republic of India is one of the world's largest **democracies**. In a democracy, the people vote to elect their leaders. Indian elections are held every five years.

In India, there is a president, but the person who has the most power is the prime minister. The prime minister helps to make new laws. There is also a Council of Ministers. The government faces difficult problems with so many different languages, more than 1000 million people and fighting between two major religious groups. Each new government tries to sort out the problems and many people feel that everything will eventually run smoothly.

INDIA'S NATIONAL FLAG

India's flag has three horizontal bars of equal width. The saffron (deep orange) colour represents the Hindus. Green represents the Muslims. The colour white represents the wish for peace between the Hindus and Muslims. The wheel in the middle is called the Ashoka chakra, which means 'wheel of justice'. The wheel is also an important symbol for the cycle of life, death and rebirth.

Religions of India

There are six major religious groups in India today. Nearly 82 per cent of Indian people are Hindu. In the Hindu religion there are many gods and goddesses, and wonderful stories about these deities telling how the world was created.

About 12 per cent of Indians practise Islam and are called Muslims. They observe the teachings of the prophet Mohammed, as written in a holy book called the Koran. Many Muslim people who lived in India moved to Pakistan when it became a separate country.

Sikhs, Buddhists, Christians, Zoroastrians and Jains make up the rest of the population. The Sikh religion is a combination of Hindu and Islamic Sufi teachings. Buddhists and Jains believe strongly in non–violence towards all living things. Buddhism developed in northern India. Buddhists are always trying to learn more and become spiritually enlightened.

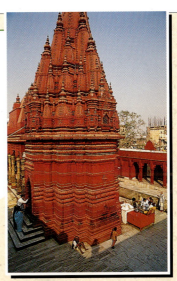

A HINDU TEMPLE ▶
Ancient temples like this are found all over India. Hindus, Buddhists and Muslims form the major religious groups.

İndian food

Because India produes so many wonderful spices, it is famous for its tasty and spicy foods, such as curries. Indian curries are dishes flavoured with a mixture of different spices. Not all curries are hot – there are also mild creamy dishes made with coconut milk. The mixture is used to cook meat, fish or vegetables. Rice, lentils and vegetables are cooked in a variety of sauces and make up a large part of the Indian diet. Home-made breads come in all shapes and sizes. Some are big and flat like dinner plates.

Many people in India are vegetarian and do not eat any meat. Followers of Hinduism and Buddhism believe in **reincarnation** so they do not eat animals. In Hinduism, cows are sacred.

If you go to a bazaar, you should try a samosa. These are little pastry pockets filled with peas, potatoes and spices, and sometimes meat or vegetables. To cool off, try a drink called a mango lassee.

◄ **INDIAN SNACKS**
Samosas are pastry pockets
stuffed with vegetables. They
make a perfect snack.

India's recipe

KHEER: NORTH INDIAN RICE PUDDING

INGREDIENTS:

950 ml milk

70 g rice, preferably long-grain
   Basmati rice

25 g sugar

4 cardamom seeds, crushed

1 tsp pistachio nuts, sliced

1 tsp raisins

A few strands of saffron soaked
   in a little milk

WARNING:

**Never cook or bake by yourself.
Always ask an adult to help you in
the kitchen.**

DIRECTIONS:

**First, rinse and soak the rice in a little water for about
30 minutes. Grind the rice with just enough water in which it
was soaked to make a fine paste. Set aside. Next, pour the
milk into a large saucepan and bring to the boil on medium
heat. Let it simmer. Meanwhile, pour a little of this hot milk
into a bowl. Add the rice paste. Add this to the simmering
milk and mix, stirring continuously. Cook on a low heat for
12 minutes or until the mixture thickens. Then add the sugar
and stir well over a low heat for about 4 minutes. Remove
from the heat. Add the saffron and raisins and sprinkle the
cardamom powder on top. Garnish with sliced pistachios.
Serve chilled.**

Up close: Bollywood

Bollywood is India's answer to Hollywood. It is based in the city of Mumbai. Films have always been very popular in India. Indian writers and film-makers are often influenced by western movies, but also add India's rich tradition of music and singing. Bollywood films have a flavour all their own.

The rise of Bollywood

In the 1940s, Indian films were black and white and often very depressing. The stories were usually sad tales about families breaking up or disasters like monsoons. Yet the music from these films became famous. Many people really enjoyed the dramas.

Over the years, large numbers of Indians have moved out of India in search of jobs. These Indians miss their homes so to stay connected with their homeland, they like to watch Indian films.

The invention of video has helped India's film industry. Films on videotape are easily shipped all over the world. As more Indians move around the globe, so do Indian films.

▲ **WHO DOESN'T LOVE A GOOD FILM?**
Bollywood billboards and posters decorate many of India's busy cities.

Bollywood today

Visiting the set of a Bollywood film is not easy. Even though Bollywood is much smaller than Hollywood, the sets are always closed to the public.

The 2002 Bollywood Awards were held in New York and were attended by top stars from India and the USA. This award show is more like a concert. Celebrities perform song and dance routines before they give out the awards.

India has become famous for its films. Many people buy the film soundtracks and enjoy listening to the Indian style of singing. Stars like Madhuri Dixit and Amitabh Bachchan are known all over the world. Indian films are particularly popular in Africa, the United Kingdom and the USA.

▲ **IT'S SHOWTIME**
Indian films are famous for their musical numbers. Dancers combine eastern and western styles of moving to lively Indian pop music.

▲ LIGHTS, CAMERAS, ACTION!
Bollywood movies have it all. Songs, dancing and always a
good dramatic story.

Holidays

There are many national and religious holidays celebrated in India. One national holiday is Independence Day which falls on 15 August. Republic Day is another. It celebrates India's first independent **constitution** and is on 26 January. Indians also celebrate the birthday of Mahatma Gandhi on 2 October. Gandhi helped India gain independence from Britain.

Holi and Diwali are two Hindu religious holidays that are fun and exciting for people of all ages. Holi is in February or March. It is the festival of colour, and marks the end of winter and the colour of spring.

Diwali takes place in October or November and lasts for several days. It is the festival of lights. It celebrates gods and mythical heroes. During this special time, people share sweets. They use fireworks and lights to keep the darkness away.

▲ **HOLI**
On the holiday called Holi, friends celebrate by throwing coloured water and harmless coloured powders on each other.

Learning the language

English	Hindi	How to say it
Hello	Namaste	nah-muh-STAY
My name is ___	Mera nam hai ___	MEH rah NAHM HAY
How are you?	Ap kese hoi	AHP KAY-say HO
I am ___ years old	May ___ sal ki hui	MAY___ SAL KEY HU
See you later	Phir milengai	FIHRR mee-len-GHAY

Quick facts

India

Capital
New Delhi

Borders
Pakistan (NW)
China, Bhutan, Nepal (N)
Myanmar (NE)
Bangladesh (E)
Bay of Bengal (E)
Arabian Sea (W)
Sri Lanka (SE)

Area
3,287,590 sq km
(1,269,338 sq miles)

Population
1,045,991,145

Largest cities
Mumbai (18,100,000 people)
Kolkata (12,900,000)
Delhi (11,700,000)
Chennai (6,000,000)

◀ **Main religious groups**

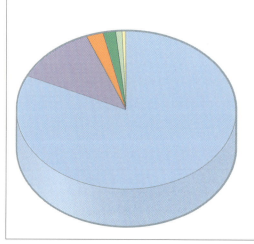

Hindu 82%
Muslim 12%
Christian 2.5%
Sikh 2%
Buddhist 0.9%
Jain 0.5%
Zoroastrian 0.1%

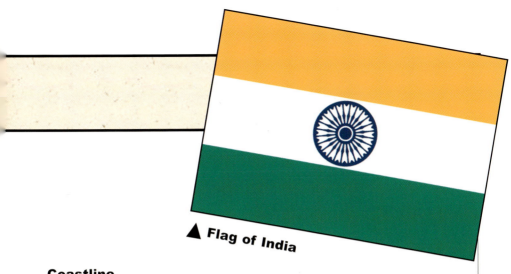

▲ Flag of India

Coastline
7000 km (4350 miles)

Longest river ▶
Ganga
2510 km (1560 miles)

Literacy rate
52% of all Indians
can read

Major industries
Chemicals, textiles,
food processing, steel

Main crops
Rice, wheat, oilseed, cotton

Natural resources
Coal, iron ore, manganese,
mica, bauxite

◀ **Monetary unit**
Rupee

People to know

Many people helped to make India great. Look at the examples below to learn who some of these people are.

◄ Mohandas Gandhi

Known as the Mahatma, Gandhi led the first non–violent demonstration for peace. Gandhi tried to help India gain independence from Britain. He was murdered in 1948. His birthday, 2 October, is a national holiday.

Indira Gandhi ►

Not related to the Mahatma, Indira Gandhi became prime minister after the death of her father, Jawaharlal Nehru, who was prime minister before her. She served in office twice. Indira Gandhi was assassinated by her bodyguards in 1984.

◄ Ravi Shankar

Ravi Shankar is a world–famous musician. He plays the sitar, a traditional Indian instrument. In the 1960s, he became popular among rock 'n' roll musicians, and particularly with the Beatles. Shankar still lives in India, in the city of Agra.

More to read

Do you want to know more about India? Take a look at the books below.

Nations of the World: India, Anita Dalal
    (Raintree, 2003)
Learn all about India and its people by exploring the history, geography and culture of this fascinating nation.

Continents: Asia L. Foster
    (Heinemann Library, 2002)
Learn about the weather, languages, animals, plants and famous places in India and other countries in Asia.

World Beliefs and Cultures: Buddhism, Hinduism, Islam, Sikkhism, Sue Penney (Heinemann Library, 2000)
Learn about the history, sacred texts, worship, festivals, pilgrimage and family life of major religions in India.

A World of Recipes: India, Julie McCulloch
    (Heinemann Library, 2001)
Learn how to cook hot and spicy dishes from India, as well as cool and refreshing ones.

Holy Places: The Ganges, Vicky Parker
    (Heinemann Library, 2002)
Explore the secrets of the river Ganga (Ganges) and the holy places along its banks. Discover why millions of Hindus make a pilgrimage to its banks.

Glossary

architecture type of design and method used to construct a building

artefact thing made and used by people

canopy in a tree, the covering or shelter created by its leaves and branches

Caste system social system that says a person's social class can never be higher than that of the family into which he or she was born

civilization society with a high state of cultural, political, social and intellectual development

constitution system of laws and government of a country

culture way of life and values of a particular society or civilization

democracy form of government in which the people vote for their government officials

economy system by which a country distributes its goods and services

empire country or large area ruled by an emperor or empress

endangered at risk of dying out

epic long, old story about heroic adventure and battles

ethnic group people of a particular race

export send products to a foreign country for sale

found to start or set up something

heritage values and customs that are handed down from generation to generation

illiteracy state of being unable to read and write

import bring items into a country from another place for sale

influence effect of one person or thing on another

lagoon shallow lake separated from the sea by a narrow strip of land such as a sand bank or reef

mausoleum large building that houses a tomb

monsoon strong wind that changes direction according to the season, bringing torrential rain from the sea

pilgrimage trip to a holy place for worship

reincarnation to be reborn into another body

republic form of government without a monarch in which the people vote for their government officials

revolt when people rise in opposition to something

sacred associated with a religion and therefore entitled to the highest respect

Sanskrit ancient literary language of India

sitar (SIT-ahr) classical Indian multi-string instrument, like a guitar with a longer neck

textile cloth or fabric

trading post store in a remote area where people can exchange goods for supplies

Vedic tradition the most ancient Hindu religious writings, in Sanskrit

Index